Including The 10 Biggest Mist...

I0058731

WHAT **REALLY** CREATES BRAND-BUILDING VIDEOS THAT GET RESULTS

From **LACKLUSTER** To **BLOCKBUSTER**

Debz Collins

Bestselling Author & Video Communications Strategist

From Lackluster to Blockbuster

*What REALLY Creates Brand–Building
Videos That Get Results*

From Lackluster to Blockbuster
What REALLY Creates Brand–Building Videos
That Get Results

Editor: Lise Bennett
Illustrator: Terri Caston

Published by Concept2Value LLC
2885 Sanford Ave SW #12965
Grandville, MI 49418 USA

ISBN: 978-0-9909532-0-3
Version 1

*Dedicated to my family and friends for
their lifetime of love and support.*

And a big thanks to Lise Bennett who shared her editing talent
and connected me with my illustrator, Terri Caston.

Praise For *From Lackluster to Blockbuster* & Debz

"Debz Collins has been a vital member of our live event video production team since 1997. She is highly skilled at what she does, always goes the extra mile and finds a way to continue to add value to our visual production."

– Robbins Research International, Inc.
An Anthony Robbins Company

"Welcome to the Visual Age. To reach your perfect audience, you must now communicate with visual impact. In FROM LACKLUSTER TO BLOCKBUSTER, Debz Collins teaches you how – giving you the same system used by her superstar clients. Invaluable!"

Ray Edwards
RayEdwards.com

"It's easy to intuitively grasp how important the technical aspects of production are to the quality of a video message. The Wisdomography PRISM framework goes further, making it clear how critical the planning and pre – production stages are to intentionally crafting an effective video that generates the desired results.

"Debz Collins really understands influence and video production. Take the time to answer the questions posed in her book and your videos will uniquely differentiate you from your competition. A thought – provoking, easy read with a clear action path to results."

Arnie Sparnins,
Retired Principal Engineer,
Intel Corporation

"There are hundreds of books out there that can tell you how to shoot a video. From Lackluster to Blockbuster explains how to shoot a video that will bring the results you desire. Debz, with 20 years of experience in video and media marketing for top level influencers, takes you beyond the lens to help you clarify your purpose, distill your wisdom, target your audience, and send the quality of visual communication you want into the world.

"If you are new to video marketing or want to increase the value of your video presence, I recommend that you pick up this book before you ever pick up your camera."

Dr. Lise Naugle, N.D.

"From Lackluster to Blockbuster is the ULTIMATE guide for taking brand – building videos from boring to soaring! Debz Collins shares the REAL secrets that allowed her to produce amazing results for Mark Victor Hansen and Tony Robbins.

"Don't wait to discover her powerful system to enhance your authority branding, build relationships and increase revenue and avoid costly mistakes along the way! Grab this book NOW!"

Ken McArthur
Best – Selling Author of *Impact: How to Get Noticed, Motivate Millions and Make a Difference in a Noisy World*
www.kenmcarthur.com

About the Author

"The beginning is the most important part of the work."

– Plato

Debz Collins is a Video Branding Strategist, documentary filmmaker and visual storyteller. She has coordinated the visual presentation and the high – end, complex video communications needs for the top speakers and trainers in the world for over two decades.

Debz is best known for her work with Tony Robbins, providing multimedia, photography, video production and video editing for Tony Robbins' live events serving 100 – 12,000+ participants in more than 140 events on five continents around the world.

Through her work with Mark Victor Hansen and Tony Robbins she had the opportunity to work with people like Deepak Chopra, Norman Schwarzkopf, Carolyn Myss, Jay Abraham, Joseph McClendon III, Kathy Buckley, Keith Cunningham, Oprah Winfrey's production team and many others too numerous to mention.

And after more than twenty years of creating visual magic as a video and multimedia professional for these top internationally known personal development and business experts, Debz has stepped out from behind the camera to share her market – making secrets with you.

Debz helps you (experts, authors, speakers and thought leaders) enhance your authority branding, build relationships and increase revenue by distilling your knowledge into a wisdom – level message and developing video – based communications systems that increase your perceived value, engage your audience and move them to action.

I AM A VISUAL COMMUNICATOR. I COMMUNICATE VISUALLY THROUGH STILL & MOVING IMAGES. I DO NOT POINT AND SHOOT. I INTENTIONALLY CRAFT A GRAPHIC, PHOTOGRAPH OR VIDEO TO CONVEY AN PURPOSEFUL MESSAGE: WHETHER IT BE INSPIRATIONAL, INFORMATIONAL, TRANSFORMATIONAL OR JUST THE BEAUTY OF THIS MOMENT. I CREATE STILL AND MOVING IMAGES TO PIQUE YOUR INTEREST, ENGAGE YOUR ATTENTION, SIMPLIFY THE COMPLEX, CREATE MOMENTS OF FOCUS, ENHANCE UNDERSTANDING AND ELICIT EMOTIONAL RESPONSES. I BELIEVE THE LEGACY OF OUR WORK IS NOT ABOUT THE QUANTITY, RATHER THE QUALITY. THE VALUE OF OUR BRANDS, OUR HEARTS AND OUR VISIONS IS REFLECTED BY THE QUALITY OF OUR COMMUNICATIONS. IT IS NOT THE INVESTMENT IN PRODUCTION GEAR THAT MATTERS, IT IS THE QUALITY OF OUR CONTENT, OUR PREPARATION AND HOW WE USE THE GEAR WE HAVE TO ITS HIGHEST POTENTIAL. CREATING HIGH QUALITY COMMUNICATIONS IS THE ONLY WAY TO BREAK THROUGH THE BARRAGE OF MEDIA WE ARE ALL BATTERED WITH EVERYDAY TO GET OUR MESSAGE SEEN, HEARD AND, MOST IMPORTANTLY, FELT. **WHEN WE EFFECTIVELY COMMUNICATE OUR WISDOM, WE CAN CHANGE THE WORLD**. AND THAT IS WHY I AM DRIVEN TO SHARE MY VISUAL COMMUNICATIONS WISDOM, ALONG WITH THE WISDOM OF OTHERS THAT HAVE INSPIRED ME. MY MISSION IS TO HELP YOU CLARIFY YOUR MESSAGE, VISUALLY ENHANCE YOUR BRAND AND SPREAD YOUR WISDOM AROUND THE WORLD. *Debz*

WISDOMOGRAPHY®

Before we begin...

First of all, thanks for picking up your copy of *From Lack-luster to Blockbuster: What REALLY Creates Brand – Building Videos That Get Results.*

Historically, this information has been shared only with my private clients along with a special "members area" of my site where I occasionally add extra content (graphics, video, audio interviews, etc.). Since you purchased this via another channel, I'm not able to offer you this supplemental material automatically.

If you are interested in taking a look additional resources and templates, head over to this special page on my website where you will find instructions on how to get access: wisdomography.com/prism-resources. You don't have to, of course – only if it piques your interest!

One more thing... Technology and the Internet will never stand still. While I may be describing what is currently available in the world of video, know that it's possible for this text to not reflex the current state of visual/video creation tools or what is happening today on the Internet. The Wisdomography.com website will always have the most up to date information. Be sure to check it out regularly.

Throughout this book, I'll be referring you to resources that can save you time, money, stress or all three. There is a page on my website where you can find all of the links and recommendations referenced in the text (so I don't have to worry about links changing in the printed text). The online resources page is located at wisdomography.com/prism-resources.

Oh, and as you may or may not be aware, I'm not able to respond to reviews left for this book in the various bookstores. If you have any problems with this publication or its contents, please contact me directly by emailing books@wisdomography.com and I'll do absolutely everything I can to get things straightened out. Thanks!

This book will challenge you with many questions. Great questions are more valuable than a book full of answers. Answers will change as technology changes and as you move through different stages in your business, but the same questions will still be valuable to guide you to the best answers for you in the present moment.

To get the most value from this book, set aside some "thinking time" to write down your answers to the questions in each chapter. Invest some time in your business to develop a solid video branding and communications strategy. Revisit the questions and your answers annually to keep your video branding and communications strategy on track.

My goal in writing this book is two-fold:

First, to empower experts and thought leaders to maximize their impact by using the Wisdomography® P.R.I.S.M™ framework to transform their message into a unique Signature Communications System.

Second, to inspire busy experts and thought leaders to build their platform and enhance their brand using the exponential power of video.

Empower & Inspire

My wish is to become your trusted advisor. I look forward to hearing your success stories as you work through the chapters of Wisdomography® P.R.I.S.M.™ You can reach me at wisdomography.com/contact.

And now, onward…

Contents

"The aim of art is to represent not the outward appearance of things, but their inward significance."

– Aristotle

Preface

"I found I could say things with color and shapes that I couldn't say any other way – things I had no words for."

– Georgia O'Keeffe

Do you have visual impact?

It's a visual world we live in. Not only are we accustomed to watching television, but we're also inundated with You-Tube videos, infographics, images and videos on Facebook, Instagram, and a plethora of other visual stimuli. Most of it is carefully crafted to communicate a specific message, often a marketing or branding message.

The question is... are you competing in the world of visual media? It used to be that the visual representation of your company, while important, was not crucial to your success. You could survive on content, skill, and talent alone.

This is no longer the case. While content, skill, talent, and results are still vital elements to the success of your business or your service practice, the truth is in the Internet age, if you are not using video to represent your material and yourself in a powerful impactful way, your business will suffer – perhaps even not survive.

The world is constantly changing. MTV began the

transition in the 1980's with their fast – cut editing techniques, and quickly in the course of a few years the attention span of the American public began to diminish. Enter Twitter, Facebook, Tumblr, Vine and Pinterest. Have you noticed that as each year passes, more and more new media sites are all emphasizing video?

Our attention has been shrunk not to 140 characters, but to a single image. You have the opportunity – and perhaps one opportunity only – to capture the imagination and the attention of your potential prospects and customers, and you must do it with video – the most sensory rich medium available.

The challenge is you must also communicate. Both effectively and with intent.

Presenting a compelling video really isn't that difficult these days. You can capture a video on your smartphone, but the question is does the video you create represent and communicate your message powerfully in a way that serves you and serves your business?

For most businesses and entrepreneurs, the answer is no. Most are not even aware that they need to have mastery of video communication techniques in the first place.

In 1978, Konica introduced the first point and shoot camera so you could take photographs without knowing anything about photography. This "advancement" in camera technology opened the door to photography for the masses. Although the point and shoot camera made it possible for you to take a decent snapshot, it didn't automatically help you craft a great photograph.

And that's where we are today in the field of videography. There are many low cost, high definition video cameras (yes, even your smartphone) that can capture a decent image with minimal technical knowledge. But just powering up your camera, hitting record and capturing a video does not make it effective, engaging, or ensure that it gets the results you want in your business.

That's where I come in. And why I created Wisdomography® – a set of systems and tools to help business owners, experts and thought leaders distill and record their unique wisdom so that it can be efficiently and effectively shared with their audience. Your wisdom is worthless if it remains trapped in your mind. However, effectively communicated, your wisdom can have massive impact for your audience.

I've been working as a video producer, documentary filmmaker, visual storyteller and Video Branding Strategist for over two decades. I've had the privilege of coordinating the visual presentation and the high – end, complex video communications needs for the top speakers and trainers in the world, developing my visual storytelling and communications mastery by working with the best.

Most of these opportunities have come through my work with names you may recognize – Tony Robbins and Mark Victor Hansen. Through Tony I've had the opportunity to work with people like Deepak Chopra, Norman Schwarzkopf, Carolyn Myss, Jay Abraham, Joseph McClendon III, Kathy Buckley, Keith Cunningham, Oprah Winfrey's production team and many others too numerous to mention.

After more than two decades of creating visual magic as a video and multimedia professional for these top internationally – known personal development experts, I'm stepping out from behind the cameras to share my branding and market – making secrets with you.

How I Help People Like You

Using the lens of my experience – in event video production, video interviews, speaker promo interviews, documentary filmmaking, photography, graphic design, and marketing with clients large and small – I've discovered how to help people shorten their learning curve to creating great video and other visually – enhanced communications that enhances your brand, engages your audience and produces a solid return on investment for your time and your money.

Historically, I've worked one – on – one with individuals looking for the highest level of personal service to help them develop a unique "Category of One" message using my proven Wisdomography® P.R.I.S.M.™ Framework.

I then create a video marketing strategy reflecting their business brand and what makes them great and takes this 'category of one' message and illustrates it in high quality videos that move people to action.

In this book I am sharing the Wisdomography® P.R.I.S.M.™, my trademarked framework. Applying this framework to your videos will raise your effectiveness in:

- Establishing a high value brand,

- Propelling yourself towards building your tribe (people who resonate with your message and what you have to offer),

- Helping more people and making more money.

While not the same as my one – on – one coaching and consulting, or even working with me in a workshop, this system is my "secret salsa" that allows me to distill your unique wisdom, knowledge, and experience into a one – of – a – kind package that makes you unduplicatable and allows you to create your own category. You will no longer have to worry about competition, because you won't have any.

I developed the Wisdomography® P.R.I.S.M.™ from my unique perspective over the last two decades through my work with top leaders, speakers, authors, and coaches – witnessing, contributing to, and even in some cases shaping the visual communication strategies of these change agents.

Now you have access to this same wisdom and perspective and the ability to apply this framework to your business. That's what the rest of this book is about. So get ready to learn how to present your unique message visually – particularly on video – in a way that powerfully transforms people and dramatically improves your results.

Chapter 1

Choosing the Lens Through Which Others See You

"In order to carry a positive action we must develop here a positive vision."

– Dalai Lama

Every one of us sees reality through our own lens. We view a particular person or situation or scenario and we quickly reach a conclusion as to what the meaning and value of that person, situation or scenario might be.

We do this in a split second. Malcolm Gladwell calls this "thinking without thinking" in his book *Blink*.

This may seem frightening because:

- You feel you don't have much control over what people think about you or

- You feel that people will instantly form a set of judgments about you and your company that may or may not be fair.

This is actually good news!

Why? Because I believe you can take control of the perceived value of your message, business, product or service by distilling your unique wisdom, knowledge, and experience into a one – of – a – kind Signature System that makes you unduplicatable using the Wisdomography® P.R.I.S.M.™.

How important is it for you to:

- Get noticed?

- Attract your tribe of raving fans?

- Become *the* brand everyone associates with your market?

What would it mean to your profitability if you had the brand recognition of Google or Fed Ex, where your name was used as a verb on a daily basis? How often have you heard someone or even yourself suggest "googling it" in reference to online searching? Have you told someone you will "Fed Ex it" to have a package shipped overnight (even if you end up sending the package through UPS)?

Brands become leaders in their field because they establish a level of trust with their customers. They add value to customers' lives and deliver on their promises.

"A lack of trust and face – to – face interaction prevents many people from purchasing online."

– Peter De Vries & Ad Pruyn, Marketing Psychologists

While face – to – face interaction with a prospect or customer may be the best way to build trust, it requires a lot of your time and money and makes it virtually impossible to reach millions of people quickly. Video, on the other hand, is a cost – effective way to put yourself in front of your targeted audience and let them get to know you.

In fact, connecting through high quality, live, on – camera video is the most powerful and cost – effective medium for sharing your wisdom, establishing trust with a large audience and building your brand. (I'll talk more about this in Chapter 7)

An online video allows you to establish a "meaningful conversation" with your prospects and customers, no matter where they live or how many there are. It gives you the best return on your investment of time and money and is the quickest way for you to add value, build your brand and become the leader in your market.

Unfortunately, as video production has become accessible to everyone, the proliferation of poorly conceived, poorly made, and time wasting video has exploded on the Internet. Your message has to compete with all of that noise for your audience's limited attention.

"There are no rules in filmmaking. Only sins!
And the cardinal sin is dullness."

– Frank Capra, Legendary Film Director

Video, unlike audio – based podcasts, requires complete attention to consume the content. If you have not clarified your unique message, you will not be able to effectively connect with your audience and inspire them to join your tribe. The first step in creating video that engages your audience is to establish your Signature System for communicating your message.

Let's begin with the theory and science behind my Wisdomography® P.R.I.S.M.™ framework. It is my framework for communications mastery and is based on the difference between mere data, information, or even knowledge and true wisdom. It is what will help you take your message/content and ultimately your videos from lackluster to blockbuster.

While data, information, knowledge, and wisdom may sound interchangeable, there is a definitive difference between those four realms of content.

This framework is not very well–known, but it's been around for quite some time. It's often referred to as the DIKW Pyramid, and it points out the basic need for a mechanism for producing new frameworks, ways of thinking about certain realms of knowledge. There are four levels of content, and the least valuable level is the one at the bottom.

This pyramid, incidentally, is also known variously as the DIKW Hierarchy, the Wisdom Hierarchy, and the Knowledge Hierarchy, as well as the Knowledge Pyramid. These terms refer loosely to a class of models that represent structural and functional relationships between data, information, knowledge, and wisdom.

The DIKW Pyramid

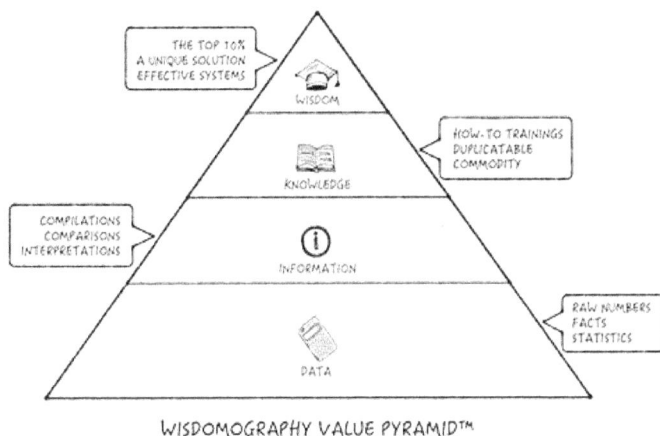

WISDOMOGRAPHY VALUE PYRAMID™

Let's talk briefly about how you are going to use this hierarchy in your search for more powerful video – based impact and communication.

The first level of content is mere data.

Data

For instance, if I tell you that there are 3500 calories in one pound of fat, that is a data point. It may or may not be interesting to you, but it has little value outside that.

Information

The next level of content is information. This means I have begun to assemble data points into a meaningful structure, such as "There are 48 calories in a small banana and 80 calories in a small apple ." Again, this may or may not be interesting, and it has negligible value unless you're choosing a fruit to eat based on calories.

Knowledge

The third level of content is knowledge. This is where you organize structures into logic chains, and you begin to use information to make conclusions and predictions. We call this realm "knowledge." This is the realm of most how–to information.

In fact, this is where the developers of most how–to information stop. That's why we have so many products, books, and seminars on "How to buy a house for no money down," or "How to lose 30 pounds in 30 days," or "How to make $10,000 a month in your spare time."

These how–to systems of content are useful, but they have some disadvantages. Those disadvantages are:

1. *They are very easy to copy.* Soon this knowledge becomes spread across the internet because so many people have copied it and adopted it as their own.

2. *Large–scale copying results in commoditization.* Suddenly the competition is not based on having or not having the knowledge, it is one of having or not having the lowest price.

3. *It leads to the "sea of sameness."* If you cannot find a way to distinguish your knowledge, you're lost in an ocean of very similar products, books, and seminars, etc.

Wisdom

The final level of content is that of wisdom. For our purposes we'll define wisdom as a unique presentation of knowledge through your distinctive lens, with the visual representation that you create, so that your content/message is perceived as unique, unduplicatable, and therefore a category – of – one.

You're not competing with other people who are attempting to communicate the same message: you have a unique message all your own.

Examples of taking what is basically common knowledge and transforming it to become wisdom – level content include:

- *The 7 Habits of Highly Effective People* by Dr. Stephen Covey

- *Awaken the Giant Within* by Tony Robbins

- *The Four Hour Work Week* by Tim Ferriss

The Widomography® PRISM™ takes the broad spectrum of your wisdom and splits it into its component parts in the same way that an optical prism splits light into the various colors of the spectrum, creating a rainbow. This enables you to focus on the individual structures and content needed to create your Signature System, allowing you to produce videos that enhance your brand and get results in a way no one else can duplicate.

The Two Realms of Wisdomography

The creation of something new is not accomplished by the intellect but by the play instinct acting from inner necessity. The creative mind plays with the objects it loves.

– Carl Jung

The Wisdomography® P.R.I.S.M.™ consists of five components. Each of these components can be further sub – divided into two realms of representation – the internal and the external. You might want to think of these as the inner game and the outer game of Wisdomography.

The "inner game" serves as a tool to help you break through the barriers that prevent you from achieving the level of success you want with your message.

The "outer game" of the framework serve as a tool for developing your communication into a powerful framework that sets you apart in the marketplace, and accelerates the acceptance of your message. It helps you transform your message into a meaningful Signature System that produces profits for you and for your clients.

The Inner Game

The internal steps of the Wisdomography® P.R.I.S.M.™ are broken down into the following *Internal* components.

Purpose

Why are you attempting to communicate this particular message? What is your ultimate outcome? What difference will it make in your life?

Resistance

What perceived obstacles prevent or oppose your presenting the message? What stands in your way? What internal blockages keep you from doing what you know you need to do in order to succeed with spreading your message successfully?

What disempowering belief do you have about promotion, marketing, packaging, money, and people that might stand in the way of your ultimate success?

Influence

What psychological triggers, anchors, or associations positively or negatively impact your behavior when you think about presenting your message? Are you uncomfortable speaking in front of people? Do you have confidence or do you fake it?

Systems

What psychological structures can you put into place that will ensure the consistent, reliable, and dependable creation and/or presentation of your own message?

What psychological hurdles do you need to clear in order to do this in a way that's efficient, effective and serves your greater purpose and mission?

Money

What are the internal associations that either attract or repel money to you? Do you have beliefs that prevent you from making as much money as you're capable of? Do you have beliefs that cause you to be in a constant state of financial distress, debt, and desperation? How can you change those internal associations?

That's the inner game.

The Outer Game

What about the outer game, the game that you play with the world? The *External* steps or outer game are as follows:

Purpose

What is the most desired result or outcome of your communications? What do you want people to do as a result of having received your communication?

Resistance

What are the possible objections or points of resistance on the part of the people you are communicating to? What would stop them from accepting or believing your message? What would stop them from acting on it?

Influence

How may you frame your content so that the people you are communicating with are most likely to consume it, understand it and act in accordance with your wishes? How can you communicate powerfully in a way that not only informs, but encourages people to action? Is the message that you are presenting in words congruent with the message you are presenting visually?

Systems

How can you establish structures that support you in producing high quality videos consistently? What video structures are necessary to enhance your brands rather than destroy them? How do you make sure your videos get noticed?

Money

How can you present your message in a way that communicates its value so that people are willing to exchange their money for your message?

Throughout the rest of this book we will examine the internal and external steps for the inner and outer game of the Wisdomography® P.R.I.S.M.™. Welcome to the rainbow.

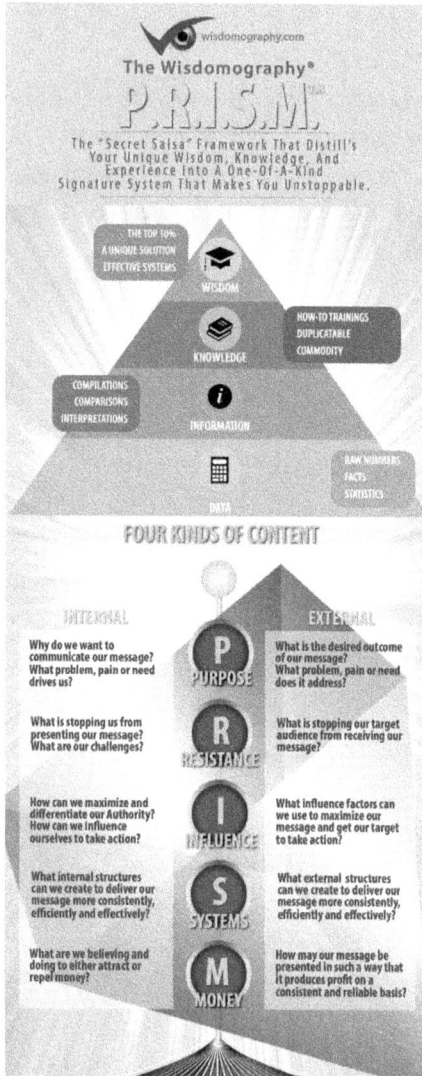

For a full – size, printable wall chart of this graphic, visit
Wisdomography.com

A QUOTE
WORTH NOTE

EVERY ONE OF US SEES
REALITY THROUGH OUR
OWN LENS.
FOCUSING YOUR
KNOWLEDGE THROUGH
YOUR LENS IS THE BEST
WAY TO REVEAL YOUR
UNIQUE WISDOM.

Debz

PURPOSE
RESISTANCE
INFLUENCE
SYSTEMS
MONEY

Chapter 2

Purpose

"Efforts and courage are not enough without purpose and direction."

John F. Kennedy

Have you ever passionately started a project only to find that when faced with obstacles you easily gave up and turned to the next bright shiny object that caught your attention?

Unless you've been trapped in an isolation tank for the last two decades, you will remember J.K. Rowling as the author of the *Harry Potter* book and motion picture series. In 1994, she had just gotten a divorce, was on government assistance, and could barely afford to feed her baby. And she was passionate about becoming a published author.

Because she couldn't afford a computer or to pay for photocopying her first 90,000 – word novel, she manually typed out each version of the *Harry Potter and The Sorcerer's Stone* manuscript to send to publishers. It was rejected dozens of times until Bloomsbury Children's Books published it in June 1997.

What made her continue writing and submitting her book

to publishers for over three years when life was so difficult and the rejections kept coming? J.K. had a strong purpose that went beyond money. She was emotionally driven to share the stories flowing in her imagination.

If you want to become a thought leader or authority in your field, you need to develop your own strong purpose to see you through the rough spots. And you need to understand your audience's purpose for seeking you out and watching your videos.

The purpose behind any of your actions is motivated by your desires. Everything you do is guided by a purpose. You always have a reason for what you do – whether conscious or subconscious.

Your reason is either to move toward a state of more pleasurable existence, or to move away from something that causes you pain.

At the most basic biological level, you want to feel good and not hurt.

It's important to understand both your personal purpose in wanting to share your message as well as your audience's purpose for consuming your communication before you begin creating videos. This is why we start with the P in the P.R.I.S.M™. system – Purpose.

Internal Purpose

It's worth asking yourself why do you want to communicate your particular message? What is your ultimate outcome? Whether you teach people how to be healthier, more financially fit, or have better relationships, or if you work in coaching and consulting relationships – there is some sort of ultimate outcome that you have for yourself in wanting to share your message.

At the surface level, you may tell yourself that purpose is monetary. You want income, but it usually goes beyond this.

Meaning is More than Money

What will cause you to keep your focus and your motivation when you begin to face obstacles and challenges in your business? It probably isn't logic. It's probably what you are planning to gain from your business communications. Money is just a means to a more satisfying end.

Certainly if you don't have money, then other things will be more problematic, but the truth is you don't really desire to have a big pile of printed government paper or large numbers in a bank account, do you?

You really want the feelings that you believe those pieces of paper (or those digital representations in your PayPal account) will bring you. You want the feeling that having a certain level of financial security brings you.

There are basic psychological human needs at work here, and it's useful to understand your own internal purpose before you figure out the external purpose of your communications. In other words, you need to deal with your own stuff before you try to deal with other people's stuff.

So what about you? Why are you in business? Why are you doing the things that you do? Why are you wanting to share your message?

All of us are trying to satisfy basic psychological human needs. Tony Robbins represents these needs as *The Six Human Needs*. (See the six boxes below for a simple explanation)

Tony Robbins: *The Six Human Needs*

1 CERTAINTY

We all have a need for certainty, security, and safety.

We want to know that things will operate a certain way, that if we step out of bed in the morning, gravity will ensure that our feet stick to the floor.

We want to have a minimum amount of money to know that we can pay our bills and provide a safe, dry, healthy place to live and food to eat for ourselves and our family.

The need for certainty often results in what social psychologists call *prevention motivation* – seeing our goals in terms of avoiding loss and keeping our life running smoothly, focusing on control to maintain the status quo.

We want to know that if we obey the rules of traffic, the other drivers won't cross the middle line and smash into us head-on, that if we deposit money in the bank, we're certain that the bank will behave honorably and treat our money with respect, and that it will still be there tomorrow.

We want to be certain.

Tony Robbins: *The Six Human Needs*

---

2 VARIETY

Seemingly in contradiction to psychological need #1 is the need for variety. If we have too much certainty we become bored with life, don't we? We simply need some variety.

This is the source of adventure, risk, mischief, and infidelity. People become so saturated by certainty that they seek variety, sometimes even resorting to harmful activities just in order to feel alive.

---

3 SIGNIFICANCE

We want to feel important and respected. Many of us believe that we're here for a purpose in life, that we have a mission to accomplish, that we're significant in the scheme of things in some way. We often satisfy this need through belonging to clubs, accumulating awards, and raising our social status.

If we feel insignificant, we may turn to unhealthy ways to satisfy our need for significance. This one explanation behind gangs, excessive material consumption and even violent crime.

Tony Robbins: *The Six Human Needs*

4 CONNECTION

None of the human needs has very much meaning if we don't feel connected to other people and to our ultimate destiny or Creator. This need for connection is not just a construct in our heads or something we feel consciously or unconsciously daily.

It's hardwired into our biology, so we're compelled to either satisfy it in a healthy way (through healthy relationships, healthy spirituality, or other means), or through unhealthy ways.

Meeting our needs for connection and/or significance leads to *promotion motivation* – seeing our goals in terms of what we can gain, or how we can end up better off. Connection and significance are often our driving force to pursue change in our situation.

5 GROWTH

It's a biological fact. There is no state that is completely static in a living creature. Either we are growing or we are receding, and if we are receding, it's the same as death. We know this instinctively. That's why we have a need, a motivation, a drive to grow and learn.

Tony Robbins: *The Six Human Needs*

6 CONTRIBUTION

This one puzzles some people, but the fact is we are also biologically wired with the need to contribute to the lives of others. To understand how important giving is, try this experiment: Take in a deep breath. Hold it, hold it, hold it. Don't let it out. Ever. Is you face blue?

It is impossible to take in air and never let it out. We must inhale and exhale. It is a requirement of life. Likewise, we must give as well as receive. And it doesn't have to be a big thing, it can be as simple as a smile or holding the door for a stranger. We contribute whenever we get out of our own heads (thinking only of ourselves) and share happiness and joy with others.

If we meet all the other needs but don't meet the need of contribution, we might be like many a high-achieving CEO whose total focus on professional success leaves him feeling unfulfilled.

Having climbed to the top of the corporate ladder, the income scale, the power scale, the societal influence scale, we'll be left asking ourselves the questions, "Is this all that there is? Is there nothing more?" Only through connection and contribution can we achieve true meaning in life.

So why is it important to identify the internal purpose?

Because if you don't understand your own internal purpose, you will self – sabotage and stop yourself from communicating in the most powerful way possible.

Why? Because your subconscious won't know how to be congruent with your actions. The brain doesn't understand why you're asking it to do the things that you want it to do, and therefore it will sit down and stubbornly refuse to do what you want. You've got to get clear on your internal purposes first.

To internally address the *Six Human Needs*, answer these questions:

1. Certainty

- What level of certainty do I have about the message I'm communicating?

- How certain am I that it will help people, that it will change lives, that it will improve society?

2. Variety

- How can I introduce variety into the way I present the message in such a way that it keeps me engaged, interested, and amused?

3. Significance

- How significant is my message really? Am I communicating a message of triviality or one of power and change?

- If I feel that my message is trivial, how might it

become significant? What might I do? How might I change the way I communicate to have a more significant message with the same outcome?

4. Connection

- How connected am I to the people to whom I'm communicating? How much do I know about them? How much do I care about them?

- How much does communicating my message increase my level of connection to them or to my Creator?

5. Growth

- In what ways does sharing my message force or encourage me to grow?

- How can I use teaching my content to help me learn even more about the subject?

6. Contribution

- What kind of contribution is my message making to the world? Am I making the world a better place by communicating this message?

- How am I helping someone beyond myself by sharing my message?

If your answers to any of these questions are unsatisfactory, it's time to sit down and work through a process of figuring out how you can make them more satisfactory, because whatever you do only has the meaning that you give it.

External Purpose

Now we move on to the external purposes of communicating your message.

At a basic level, you must first decide what result you want from your video. What are you trying to get people to do because they heard your message?

Do you want them to:

- Join your email list?

- Follow you on social media?

- Buy a product or service?

- Donate to your cause?

- Become more aware of your brand, cause, product or service?

- Trust you more?

- Recognize you as an expert or authority?

- Take action on your best tip?

- Feel better?

- Have less pain?

- Be entertained?

- Share your video?

- Be motivated or inspired to try something new?

- Watch another video?

- Call you for an appointment?

- Refer you to others?

- Send you a testimonial?

- Make a difficult decision?

- Be moved to laugh?

- Be moved to cry?

- Or ...?

The most effective videos have a single goal to achieve. Be clear and you will get the action you want. Be confusing and nothing will happen.

Let's now dig a little deeper and investigate why your audience will not only be willing to watch your video but actually seek you out. In other words, why will your audience care about your message, product or service?

Trust me, if they don't care, they won't listen, and they certainly will not act. For sure they're not going to give you their hard – earned money for a message they don't care about.

How do you ensure that people care about the message you're communicating? By focusing first on them, not on you.

You need to figure out what pain or problem your communication addresses or solves. If there is no pain or problem that you're solving, you're going to have a very difficult time of communicating a message that causes people to value what you are offering and to spend money with you.

And the more value you give, the more value you get back – the universal law of Karma. In business, the key to being successful is to always add value. For every video you create, you must ask yourself, "How am I adding value to my audience?"

Think of it this way. What needs are you fulfilling for

your audience with your communications? How can you help them fulfill all of their needs at the highest level? Let's go through the same list we've already traveled through together. Take some time now to answer these questions.

1. Certainty

- How am I communicating a level of certainty to my audience about my solution to their problem or pain? How certain can I make them that I actually know the answers that will give them the relief they seek?

- Is my message clear? Do I alleviate confusion and indecision? Am I consistent in my communications? Do I have schedules and systems in place that add to my reliability and trust?

- Do I have consistent branding for my videos: persona/identity, tone, program structure, logos, intros and outros, watermarks, music, level of quality, visual style, delivery style? Is my audience able to recognize my videos just from the video thumbnail?

The more certainty and consistency you can give them, the more attention they will give you.

2. Variety

You must present your message in a variety of different ways to keep your audience interested, engaged, and enthralled with what you have to say.

- Do I produce video in a for a variety uses: customer service, sales, case studies, professional introductions,

Web site welcomes, product demos, tips, lead generation, explainers, reviews, testimonials and more?

- Am I communicating using multiple formats: video, audio, writing, infographics, and photos? Am I using a variety of video engagements: instructing, inspiring, and entertaining; and a variety of styles: animation, screen sharing, kinetic text, direct to camera, interview, and mini – documentary? Do I know what combination gets the best result with my audience?

- Do you use pattern interrupts to reacquire their attention throughout a longer video? Do you start your videos with a curiosity builder?

Nobody likes to listen to a one – note symphony. Keep your message interesting, your formats varied, and your content new to keep your audience engaged.

3. Significance

- Does the communication of my message bring a feeling of significance to my audience? Does it make them feel important and respected? Does it show that I respect their time?

- Does my communications enhance how they value themselves? Does it cause them to connect with their higher purpose? Does it cause them to understand that they have something to contribute to society?

One way to help your audience feel more significant is to create videos and other online content that are accessible only to your VIP group through a membership site. Charging a premium price for your video content may also play to your audience's need for significance.(It should go without saying that you must over deliver on value, but I'll repeat it anyway)

Highlighting your customers' success in a video case study is another way to help them feel significant.

4. Connection

- Am I using the power of storytelling, analogies and metaphors in my video content? Have I connected with my audience emotionally? Does my body language reflect my message?

- Am I interacting with my audience through comments and social media on a consistent basis? How am I rewarding engagement?

Like it or not, you've got to create an emotional connection between you and the people you want to reach. A failure to do so is a failure of your business. How do you connect emotionally? Transparency, honesty, and the revelation of some of your own flaws and humanity are usually the best ways to make a connection with your audience.

On – camera video is very effective in creating human connection. We are all biologically hard – wired to pay attention to the human face and movement, and we are drawn to the eyes and smiles. Let your personality and heart connect through your words, voice and body language.

All communication evokes emotion (yes, boredom is an emotion). One of the most powerful ways to reach others emotionally is through the power of storytelling, analogies and metaphors, especially when you share personal stories that support your message.

Many people think of video as a one – way form of

communication. Create a two way connection by asking questions and providing a way for your audience to leave comments. Be sure to follow up by rewarding engagement and build an even stronger connection.

5. Growth

- How am I challenging my audience to grow if they accept my message?

For example, Dave Ramsey presents a message of becoming debt – free and not using credit cards to fund one's existence. This is a challenging step for most people and certainly causes them to grow in a way that can make them uncomfortable.

However, because Dave supplies his audience with certainty, because he communicates his message in a variety of different ways, underlines how they'll regain their own self respect by being debt – free, and has a connection with his audience (having been in their same exact situation), he's able to encourage them to grow through doing something that makes them uncomfortable. You must do the same.

6. Contribution

- How am I helping my audience see that they're making a contribution by following my message?

You must make a connection and join the dots between what you're teaching or sharing with people and their own feeling of contribution to their family, community or world at large. If you fail to do so, you're failing to reach your maximum profit potential with your message.

In the next chapter we'll examine why, even though you may be meeting all of your audience's needs psychologically that are required to fulfill the Purpose portion of P.R.I.S.M.™, you may still be meeting with resistance.

Why don't people say yes? Why don't they buy? Why don't they make a decision to change? We'll answer all these questions in the next chapter.

A QUOTE WORTH NOTE

PURPOSE IS THE
ULTIMATE DRIVER.
DON'T BEGIN STEERING
YOUR COMMUNICATIONS
UNTIL YOUR DRIVER IS
BEHIND THE WHEEL.

Debz

PURPOSE

RESISTANCE

INFLUENCE

SYSTEMS

MONEY

Chapter 3

The Resistance

"Never forget: This very moment, we can change our lives. There never was a moment, and never will be, when we are without the power to alter our destiny. This second, we can turn the tables on Resistance. This second, we can sit down and do our work."

Steven Pressfield

Steven Pressfield in his seminal work, The War of Art, writes about what he calls "The Resistance." He identifies it as a malevolent, almost conscious force of evil that seeks to stop us from doing our best work, from creating our art, from being productive.

Anyone who's ever tried to create anything, whether it's a video, a book, a seminar, or an audio program, knows about the Resistance.

My father's primary focus in life was the education of his children, or so it seemed when I was growing up and under constant pressure to be the best. Over time that push to be the best created a severe case of "perfectionism" disease in me.

It wasn't until I began working in corporate and event video production that I experienced the cure for perfectionism. (Okay, well maybe I'm not cured, but at least I'm in remission). I learned that no Hollywood movie, documentary, event video nor commercial video would exist if it was required to be perfect.

In event video production, your only course of action is to do your best in the heat of the moment. If you are projecting IMAG (image magnification – the live image of the presenter) and other video sources to screens, the audience sees everything you do. I soon realized that most of the time, I was the only one who even noticed what I considered to be a mistake. Once the event is over you can't go back and fix (or *perfect*) anything. It's over. Done. Fait accompli.

Pixar Movie Producer and Director, John Lasseter, has been quoted as saying "Our films don't get finished, they just get released."

There is no budget big enough or time schedule long enough to create perfection. Strive for outstanding work and you will blow away the competition. Strive for perfectionism and you will never even be a player.

Perfectionism has become one of the leading manifestations of the Resistance. And one of the toughest ones to conquer for many. We will explore perfectionism and more in this chapter.

When dealing with Resistance, you need to think about once again the internal and external forms – the inner game of Resistance and the outer game as you frame your communications and construct your videos.

The Inner Game of Resistance

What stands in the way of you presenting your message in the most compelling way possible? How does the Resistance show up for you when you're trying to frame your own communications to your own tribe?

For most of the people I've worked with, particularly related to video and film production, internal forms of Resistance show up in a variety of forms. These include:

1. Time – "I don't have enough time to work on my messaging or video production."

This is one I hear frequently. The fact of the matter is, you and I and every other human being all have exactly the same amount of time – 168 hours per week. How each of us choose to invest that time is the difference. If you really feel that time is a challenge for you, you might ask yourself a few pointed questions:

"How much time did I spend watching television this past week? How much time did I spend surfing the internet? Looking at Facebook? Playing around on cable television?" The answers may surprise you.

This is not to say that you don't need to engage in recreation. But if time is your excuse, you need to take that one off the table because we all have the same amount of time, but we don't all achieve the same level. There has to be a reason. That reason is some are choosing to spend their time differently than others.

"The easier it is to do, the harder it is to change."

Eng's Principle

If spending most of your free time playing with your dog, zoning out in front of the television or watching funny cat videos on YouTube has become a habit, it will take some effort to make a change. This is where having a strong, compelling Purpose or "reason why" comes in handy.

Remind yourself of your Purpose for being in business and wanting to share your message. When you have a compelling Purpose, the decision about what to do with any block of time will become simpler. Commit to what is important to you now so you don't wake up ten years from now in the same place.

2. Money – "I don't have enough money to invest in video production."

This is deadly. You won't make any money if you don't present yourself in a professional way that showcases and highlights your competency, your skill level, your trustworthiness, and conveys the mental and emotional image you want to express of yourself and your work. Saying that you don't have the money to invest in yourself is like saying, "I don't want any money." You don't have enough money not to invest in producing videos that communicate more effectively. End of story.

3. Technology – "I just don't understand the internet, video, Twitter, Facebook, PowerPoint, etc."

As a person who's been around high achievers for the last two decades, I can tell you that this kind of thinking doesn't serve you. Not understanding technology is no excuse. If you don't understand something, the answer is to educate yourself until you understand it or work with someone who does! Which leads to #4.

4. Knowledge – "I just don't know how."

Well, then, as you might expect, my advice is: learn how or hire an expert in that field! This is not rocket science, but it needs pointing out.

5. Perfectionism – "I can't release anything until I know it's perfect."

Hmm… you can stop reading now because you will never release your work. There is no such thing as perfect. You are really just afraid of being judged and having someone find fault with you or your message. There will always be fault finders no matter how great your message is. That's part of your human makeup. And, unfortunately, the anonymity of the Internet has made it even easier for all of us to publicly post our critical judgments without repercussion.

As my good friend, Joseph McClendon III, has shared with me, the best philosophy to have for your peace of mind and sanity is: "Your opinion of me is none of my business." Let go of worrying about other's opinions unless you believe you can learn something constructive from them.

And remember, you are your own worst enemy. You will tear yourself down mentally and emotionally much more than you would let anyone in the outside world. If you are bothered by the way you look or the sound of your voice and that is stopping you from communicating your message on video, then either do something about it or let it go. No one sees you as critically as you do. Stay focused on your Purpose and your message.

6. Other Limiting Beliefs

I encourage you to take a moment or two to write down any beliefs that you have that are holding you back that are manifestations of the Resistance, that keep you from presenting the best possible visual representation of your message.

Do you believe that you or your message doesn't deserve professional quality video production? Do you believe that people might think you're too slick? Do you believe it's too expensive to hire a graphic designer or a video production team or a coach?

Whatever the limiting belief is, you might spend some time asking yourself, "Why do I believe that?" or "What would I have to believe in order for that to be true?"

When you talk about what you want and why you want it, there's usually less Resistance within you than when you talk about how you're going to get it. Asking questions you don't have answers for, like how, where, when, who, sets up a contradictory feeling that slows everything down. That's why the P.R.I.S.M.™ framework begins with Purpose. It's what keeps you on track through the rest of the framework when the process seems difficult.

Overcoming the internal Resistance is the most important thing I can share with you in this whole book.

Only by overcoming your own Resistance will you consistently achieve the success you desire.

External Resistance

As you have probably figured out by now, we're going to spend the next part of this chapter talking about how to help your audience overcome the points of resistance that keep them from accepting your message.

As you might have predicted, they are similar to the obstacles that prevent you from presenting your message. Let's explore them.

They are:

Time – "Will this video take up too much of my time?"

Your audience is trading their limited time to watch your video. You must deliver more value in your video than they believe their time is worth. Remember, you are competing with millions of other options both online and offline for their time and attention.

The Internet Age has sped up all of our lives, adding to our impatience and leading us to expect instant gratification. For example, newer online video platforms only allow videos of 6 seconds (Vine) and 15 seconds (Instagram) in length. Our attention spans have been reduced to less than 10 seconds. If you don't communicate the value of your video and grab their attention quickly, your viewers will move on.

Recent studies by Wistia have shown that viewership drops off quickly after the first sixty seconds. To combat this, either create punchy, content rich videos of 1 minute or less or establish enough perceived value in that first 60 seconds that the majority of your viewers will watch all the way to the end.

2. Value – "Will this video make my life/business easier, more productive, more profitable or provide some other value?"

You should always strive to create significant value through your content, performance and technical production, but especially when you are charging people money to view your videos. Not enough perceived value results in high resistance to your offer and no income.

On – camera video value is derived from 50% content and structure, 30% performance delivery and 20% technical production. The higher the quality of each of these components, the more you can charge for your video – based products, and the more value you are creating for your brand.

3. Technology – "Will I be able to view this video the way that works best for me?"

How will your audience view your videos? Are they primarily computer users or mobile users? Do they prefer to buy dvd's or blu – ray disks? Do they search for content like yours on YouTube or iTunes?

To reduce your audience's resistance to viewing your message, make sure you deliver it the way they want it. If you don't have enough information about your audience's preferences, provide your video in all formats and on all platforms.

4. Complexity – "Will I be able to understand what is being shared?"

This can be the curse of being an expert. You know your subject so well that you forget to make a complex or advanced subject simple enough for a beginner to grasp.

The highest value you can provide is to take a complex concept and make it simple. No one wants to watch a video that makes them feel stupid or confused.

You need to think like a non – expert… remember what it was like when you were starting out. Remove or explain jargon, use stories and metaphors, and add visuals to explain complex concepts.

If you are struggling with reducing complexity, be sure to share the content for your next video with several non – experts. Get their feedback before you spend your time and money producing the video.

5. Lack of Trust – "Does this person (or company) really know what they are talking about? Do they really care about me or just getting my money?"

"I don't trust you/ the organization." At this level people respond not to the validity of your message per se but to the one who is suggesting it.

Start immediately to develop trust through on – camera video so your audience can get to know, like and trust you better by seeing your face, hearing your voice and experiencing your content on a multi – sensory level. If you have personally experienced success with your product or service, share your personal story.

Self – Esteem – "Will I be able to get similar results?"

You must show how your audience can apply what you are sharing in your video or how it will make a difference in their lives or the lives of people they care about. Some of your audience may believe that your message worked for you, but have doubts about their own ability to follow your advice and get similar results. Showing how people like them have already gotten benefits from your system or message will make them more receptive to your content.

Helping your audience overcome their points of resistance is one of the most powerful steps you can take in communicating your own message. Delivering your content in a way it can be trusted and understood and in a medium that is best suited to your specific audience will go a long way in reducing resistance.

Giving them useful "help in advance", even through your marketing materials, helps instill a high degree of confidence and certainty about who you are and what you offer.

But how do you move people from being certain about you as a person, about having belief and faith in what you're offering them, to taking action, to making a purchase, to spending money?

That's what the next chapter is all about – how to influence people in such a way that they act, how to get people to buy.

A QUOTE
WORTH NOTE

Resistance challenges
your commitment to
Purpose. Pushing
through the Resistance
forces you to grow
which makes you and
your message stronger.

Debz

PURPOSE
RESISTANCE
INFLUENCE
SYSTEMS
MONEY

Chapter 4

Influence

"Think twice before you speak, because your words and influence will plant the seed of either success or failure in the mind of another."

Napoleon Hill

One of the most powerful ways to sell products and services to people is to never have to sell them.

In fact, marketing guru Dan Kennedy says if you have to use a hard – sell approach to moving your products and services, you simply do not have enough…influence. Influence is the ability to get people to act. To cause them to do things.

There's a story of two great leaders in ancient Rome. When one of these leaders would take the podium the audience would cheer, applaud, and shout, "Hurrah!"

But when the other leader took the podium the audience would be inspired to march for a cause. You want to be the kind of communicator that causes people to act rather than merely cheer your great words. How do you do this? That's the subject of this chapter.

Internal Influence

Before you can influence anyone else, you've got to learn to influence yourself, so I'd like to encourage you to think about what's already influencing you right now.

What psychological triggers, for instance, make you angry, sad, or depressed? What songs, smells, or associations positively or negatively affect your behavior? Specifically, what psychological triggers do you have set up around communicating your message?

If the mere idea of taking the stage or appearing on live video to present your message fills you with fear, causes you to break out in a cold sweat, makes your heart rate to speed up, or your respiration to become shallow and rapid, you've got to learn to influence yourself so that trigger does not cause fear in you.

Psychological triggers that negatively impact your behavior when it comes to presenting your message can stop you from succeeding.

What you need when it comes to influencing yourself are the following:

1. Confidence in the power and validity of your own message.

If you don't believe in what you're selling, no one else is going to buy. That's only common sense, yet it's something so often passed over by people in the early stages of a business.

2. Absolute congruity.

You've got to walk your talk. You can't be one person when presenting your message and be another person when "off – stage" or "off – camera."

That kind of incongruity will catch up with you sooner or later, and most people can smell it a mile away. Don't be fake. Be congruent with your own message. Influence yourself first before you try to influence other people.

3. Rituals

What are some rituals you can do regularly to master influence over yourself? Review your Purpose for sharing your message, exercise to get oxygen flowing to your brain, read or listen to inspirational or educational books, eat a healthy diet, read testimonials from those you have already helped, listen to great music, or connect with a mentor or good friend who believes in you. What else would work for you?

4. Practice

Practice breeds confidence. If you are constantly simply winging the presentation of your message, you're going to find yourself lacking confidence. You may totally believe in your product or service, and you may actually present incredible value to the world with the service that you bring, including the ability to change lives and shape destinies. However, if you're fearful when it comes to presenting your message because you haven't practiced communicating it, the delivery of your message will not engage people to listen to what you have to say.

You've got to get this one concept deep in your core as a belief. You owe it to those you know you can help to communicate with the greatest level of influence.

If your message is true and you don't influence as powerfully as you possibly can, you are robbing people of a solution to their problem and their pain. Use your passion about spreading your wisdom and helping others to fuel your own confidence and master the external skills of influence we'll be exploring next.

External Influence

Once you've influenced yourself, you inherently will understand one of the most powerful principles of influence that exists. The easiest and fastest way to influence anyone is to use what is already influencing them.

The great marketer and copywriter Robert Collier nearly 100 years ago said that in order to write effective advertising copy we must "join the conversation already taking place in the reader's mind."

What this means to you today is you have to find a way to frame your communications in such a way that the people who are listening to you are likely to act in accordance with your wishes.

How do you do that?

1. Give results in advance.

Giving away your best ideas is often your best form of marketing. People can use those ideas to get results, and then become addicted to your messages because they want more of what worked so well and made them feel so good to begin with. Don't be afraid of using your best material as your best marketing.

2. Think strategically about your communications.

Simplicity fosters clarity. Every communication should have one single Most Desired Result. Too many times I see people trying to market five or six different messages in a single video, email, speech, or podcast.

Attempting to share three messages means that no message is remembered. It's easy to create a long rambling video, audio or blog post. It takes a lot more time and effort to hone it into a simple and profound message that will resonate with your audience.

To practice, start by creating a 60 second or less "tip" video. What are the bare essentials you need to share? Cut the fluff and you will have them coming back for more.

The fact is, every communication should have one single objective, and that objective should be your primary focus. A critical part of this objective is a singular Call to Action. (More on this in Chapter 6). A failure to be clear will confuse your audience, resulting in their failure to take action.

3. Learn to write in "headlines." (Or in the case of video, "titles")

Newspapers are good at this. Tabloid newspapers are better. Have you ever noticed how sensationalist and attention – getting the headlines are on the tabloids like The National Enquirer?

One of my favorites: "Boy Eats Own Head"

While these headlines can be bizarre, they are unexpected and attention – grabbing. Learn to frame your communications with "headlines." Here are a few examples:

- The One Weird Trick That Makes You Super Confident 100% of the Time

- The 5 Foods You Must Never Eat on an Airplane

- Are You Making These Mistakes in English?

- 7 Ways to Know If He's Cheating on You Right Now
- The 6 Most Powerful Words in the English Language, and How to Use Them to Grow Your Business

Frame your communications with headlines that grab the attention of your audience. It is a powerful and necessary step in making your communications a habit and a positive addiction for your audience.

4. Credibility

Live video is one of the quickest ways to establish trust and credibility. How you look, sound and act on video will give more clues to who you are than a blog update or even a podcast. People take advice and recommendations from those they identify with or want to be like. Be your authentic self and your tribe will find you.

Do you have past successes that add to your credibility? If not, get them. Use case studies to illustrate how your wisdom has helped others. Humanize your message. Use metaphors and anecdotes to explain complex ideas.

5. Emotions and Storytelling

All effective communication is based on emotions. You will rarely remember a lot of data and statistics or lists of features and benefits unless you are drawn into the information emotionally.

Most of us who were alive on September 11, 2001 (even if you are not American) will remember where we were that day and what we were doing because of the strong emotions attached to the events of that day. In contrast, how many of you remember where you were on August 11, 2001?

The best way to influence another person is to draw them into your message emotionally. Help them experience how great they will feel when they use your product or service. Remember, we all just want to feel good – less pain, more pleasure.

Stories that spark your audience's emotions are one of the most influential tools you can employ. Stories are a memorable way to teach, inspire, and move people to action. They draw your audience in and allow them to rehearse their future possibilities, providing a mental simulation of a future life where their current problem is solved. Stories lower their natural resistance to being influenced.

When we listen to a story, your brain is hardwired to experience the same emotions as the characters in the story. And although we all would like to think that we are completely logical beings, most decisions are emotionally based. Share a story that moves your audience from frustration or pain to inspiration or excitement and they will be primed to take action.

Now that you've influenced people to behave and consume your video content in the way that you want them to, what's next? The problem that most entrepreneurs run into is consistency and quality control in their video productions.

You need systems that do the work for you. You need to be able to work on your business instead of in your business, and that's what the next chapter is all about.

A QUOTE
WORTH NOTE

ONE OF THE MOST
POWERFUL WAYS TO
SELL PRODUCTS AND
SERVICES TO PEOPLE
IS TO NEVER HAVE TO
SELL THEM.

Debz

PURPOSE
RESISTANCE
INFLUENCE

SYSTEMS

MONEY

Chapter 5

Systems

Knowing reality means constructing systems of transformations that correspond, more or less adequately, to reality.

Jean Piaget

A system is a pre – planned way of getting things done that operates with or without your intervention. You need systems in your business to make it work better, so you can work less. McDonald's is a prime example of systems thinking.

How is it possible for a multimillion – dollar business – like a single McDonald's franchise – to operate smoothly 24 hours a day, 7 days a week, 365 days a year…run mostly by teenagers? The answer is: systems.

If you've ever worked at McDonald's you know that every single step of the operation of that restaurant is spelled out in simple easy to understand steps. Any reasonably intelligent person could step off the street, pick up one of the laminated system checklists, and run the restaurant in a short period of time.

You need systems for your video communications that are just as simple, just as direct, and just as effective.

There are a lot of moving parts to a quality video that affects it's results:

1. Concept

2. Script/Content Outline

3. Delivery/Performance

4. Technical Production:

   Audio – Microphones, Noise Reduction

   Lights

   Camera – Focus, Exposure, Movement, Support

   Location

   Wardrobe & Makeup

   Composition...

5. Editing

6. Video SEO

7. Distribution

Each of these areas has it's own list of steps. That's why systems are critical to avoid overwhelm. Getting systems in place also makes it possible to have others take over the tasks that you don't need to personally do.

Let's face it, if video production is not easy, fun and rewarding, you're not going to be consistent – in quality nor quantity.

As with all of our other letters of our P.R.I.S.M™ acronym, the S of P.R.I.S.M.™ (Systems) has two variations…

Internal Systems

Before you start creating effective and engaging videos, you have to think about your internal systems for creating quality videos, especially those related to productivity, consistency and creativity in your business.

Focus

If you know you're easily distracted by the internet, for instance, make sure when you're working on your messaging that you work in an environment where you're not internet – connected. It's as simple as that. If your cell phone is a temptation, don't take it with you to your office. Multitasking is never efficient. Stop putting the brakes on your success velocity.

If you have trouble staying focused, check out one of my favorite systems, the Pomodoro Technique by Francesco Cirillo (more info in the Resources section). This technique was developed to help you:

1. Work with Time – not against it

2. Eliminate Burnout

3. Manage Distractions

4. Create a Better Work/Life Balance

The basic idea is that you set a timer for 25 minutes of uninterrupted time to work on a specific task such as scripting a new video or actually shooting the video. When the timer reaches zero, take a short five minute break and get up, move around, exercise, or drink water. That's one "pomodoro" cycle.

Then repeat the cycle three more time and take a longer fifteen to thirty minute break. This will keep your energy up for sustained bursts of creative productivity.

As Tony Robbins often says, "The secret to happiness is progress." Not having a system to get things done and move you forward leads to frustration and unhappiness. Commit now to find a focusing system that works for you.

Consistency

Once you've made the commitment to producing videos for your business, it can be easy to put off getting started or being consistent. The process may seem daunting and time consuming. Unfortunately, making one video once a year will not do your brand much good. I'm not proposing that you produce a video everyday, but you need to have a regular, consistent schedule for releasing videos to your audience to maintain your momentum. And that means actually blocking out time on your calendar.

> *"When you talk about something, it's a dream.*
> *When you envision it, it's exciting.*
> *When you plan it, it's possible.*
> *When you schedule it, it's real."*

> – Tony Robbins

Be realistic about your time when you are starting out. Start with producing an "About" video and "Welcome" video for your Web site and then schedule to release one high quality video a week. (For video content inspiration, go to http://wisdomography.com/prism-resources) You could do less but it will take longer to get comfortable on camera if you don't make it a part of your business routine.

Every task of video production is simpler when you have a system. Setting up a dedicated studio area in your home or office and leaving the tripod, lights and microphones in place, connected and ready to go will reduce the time it takes to shoot a video. If you make it easy and efficient, you will be more likely to do it on a consistent basis.

If you don't have the space to dedicate to a studio, try scheduling a full day every couple of months to shoot ten to twenty short videos back to back that can be uploaded over a two month time period. It's all about creating a system that makes your process simpler.

Set specific goals and hold yourself accountable. Commitments to others, whether employees, outsourcers, friends or family may make you more likely to follow through than when you are only responsible to yourself.

Even if you're not prepared, if it is on your schedule, do it anyway. Avoid letting yourself off for any excuse. Doing so will just encourage your mind to find another excuse the next time. Every session in front of the camera will make you a better on-camera speaker, and your presentation could be edited for an audio podcast or transcribed for a blog post. Whether or not you choose to show the video, your time is not lost. If the video is not usable, just transform it into a content medium that is.

Find ways to make the process fun and enjoyable. Work with people that know how to produce high quality video, pull out your best performance, reduce your stress and make you laugh. If you try to do it all by yourself, the process may become a chore to avoid.

Creativity

Creative people tend to be prolific. Not every idea will fly. The best way to develop your creativity is to stop judging your ideas while you are brainstorming. Stop thinking and start writing. Get the ideas out of your head and on to physical paper.

Add artificial constraints for your creativity to push against. For example, imagine how you could tie your message to the biggest headline in today's paper or the lead story on CNN. What video could you create that would involve everyone in your business?

Creativity is the key to great video (and especially viral video). If you find it challenging to think outside the box, team up with someone who can and start flexing your creative muscles. The more you "workout" your creativity, the more you creativity will grow.

You know your areas of weakness and the psychological systems and disciplines you need to develop. Just make sure you develop structures that support your productivity, consistency and creativity.

External Systems

Establishing external systems and structures to ensure the reliable delivery of your message to large numbers of people through online video that those videos get seen by your tribe is often a little easier than creating internal systems. This is where technology becomes your friend.

There are many systems available that will deliver your message automatically, affordably, and systematically. Using the power of the internet and technologies such as live streaming events such as Google Hangouts On Air or other video delivery systems, your message can be spreading across the globe, creating new fans and making you money even while you sleep.

Having your own YouTube channel or iTunes video podcast show, for instance, can be tantamount to owning your own television network if you produce enough quality content.

Your key objective is not just to produce a large quantity of high quality video. It is to get your message/content found, seen, consumed, shared and acted upon.

1. Do you have systems, templates and checklists for creating concepts and scripts for different types of online video?

   - About/Brand videos
   - Intro or Welcome videos
   - FAQs videos
   - Sales videos
   - Product Launch videos
   - Google Hangouts On Air
   - Customer Service videos
   - Testimonials
   - Quick Tips videos
   - Weekly Series videos
   - Instructional Video Course
   - Case Study videos
   - Mini – documentaries

2. Do you have a show structure for each type of online video?

3. Do you have a system for shooting spur of the moment videos in a quality way that will support your branding?

4. Do you have a system for shooting brand critical videos regularly and efficiently?

5. Do you have systems for automated sales and distribution of your video content in place?

6. Do you have systems for quality outsourcing as much of the pre – production, production and post – production as you can so you can get more done?

7. Do you have systems for distributing your videos online so that they will be discovered and seen?

8. Do you have a system for measuring and tracking your video's results so you can maximize your return on investment?

If you answered "no" to any of the questions above, go to wisdomography.com/prism – resources for free access to some of the resources I currently use for my clients and in my own business.

Having a powerful message is not enough if you truly want to have an impact. The key is to build systems that allow the consumption of your wisdom – of your unique knowledge and experience – without reinventing the wheel each time you want to create a video.

Once you have your messaging in place and it's being delivered with consistent quality through the use of systems in your business, the goal is to turn it into money? I'll show you how in the next chapter.

A QUOTE
WORTH NOTE

YOU NEED SYSTEMS
IN YOUR BUSINESS
TO MAKE IT WORK
BETTER, SO YOU
CAN WORK LESS.

Debz

PURPOSE
RESISTANCE
INFLUENCE
SYSTEMS
MONEY

Chapter 6

Money

"Money won't create success, the freedom to make it will."

Nelson Mandela

It's been said that money cannot buy happiness, but that it can provide a luxurious lifestyle in which you can enjoy your unhappiness in relative comfort.

While we all know instinctively that money in itself does not deliver happiness, we all also know instinctively that the miseries caused by not having money distract us from the ultimate fulfillment we seek in life. These are barriers and hurdles we must get past.

Unless you are already financially independent and have no need for more money, you must make this a focus or your message will never reach it's destiny. No matter how big your heart is and how much you want to help others, ignoring your own financial needs will eventually lead you to abandoning your quest to spread your message.

Let's examine the psychological challenges both you and your clients have with money.

Internal Money Game

What are your internal associations that either attract or repel money? You have them, whether you're aware of them or not. See if you can complete any of the following phrases:

- Money doesn't grow on…

- A penny saved is a penny…

- Pennywise and …

- Money can't buy…

If you can complete those phrases, you've proven that you've already been pre – programmed to have some disempowering beliefs about money. Many of us were raised in an environment that taught us the "zero – sum game" model of reality.

The participants of this game believe that for some to have more, others must have less. In other words, there are winners and there are losers. If we use the analogy of the economy being like a pie, we believe that if we get a bigger piece of pie, there's less pie for everyone else. This leads to a scarcity mindset where we believe there are limited resources.

The opposite of the scarcity mindset is the prosperity mindset or abundance mindset. This way of thinking isn't limited by the size of the pie. It simply solves the problem by baking more pies and making them bigger.

Dealing with your own internal mind triggers and associations related to money is very important. Take a few moments right now to do the following exercise:

1. Set a timer and for the next 5 minutes write continuously about everything you can think of related to money. Don't let your pen stop, just keep it moving

and keep writing down every association, phrase, thought, belief, or challenge you have when it comes to the subject of money. They could be positive or they could be negative. You just want to keep pouring those thoughts out of your brain until you feel you've emptied everything out.

2. Now go back and look at what you just wrote and ask yourself, "Do I really want to believe this? Does it really serve me?" For the beliefs that don't serve you, draw a line through them right now. Cross them off. Decide right now that you're not going to accept those beliefs anymore.

3. Nature abhors a vacuum, so if you simply say, "I'm not going to believe something anymore," inevitably that belief will return unless you replace it with a different belief. For the beliefs that you chose to let go of you need to come up with an alternative empowering belief to replace it. For instance, if you chose to no longer believe "Money doesn't grow on trees," you might replace it with "God (or the Universe) supplies me abundantly with all the money I need, based on the value that I create in the world."

This is a long process and goes beyond the scope of this book, but this should get you started. If you are ready for more, check out "Wired for Wealth: Change the Money Mindsets That Keep You Trapped and Unleash Your Wealth Potential" by financial psychologists Drs. Brad Klontz and Ted Klontz and financial planner Rick Kahler, CFP.

You've got to deal with your own internal baggage about money if you really want to make as much of it as possible.

I also highly recommend the work of my friend and colleague, Keith Cunningham, who can really help you get a grasp money and business. You will get a lot of value from reading Keith's book, *Keys to the Vault* and *The Ultimate Blueprint for an Insanely Successful Business.*

The bottom line: if you are not comfortable with money and asking others to value and purchase your product or service, it will come across on your video and in all of your communication.

External Money Game

The external money game is really more of a mechanical exercise. You need to learn the ways to present your message to the world so that it produces profit on a consistent and reliable basis. This means communicating in ways that result in sales.

This is where many people get tripped up. They don't want to be thought of as "sales – y." It's not necessary to be a sales person or to be pushy or hype – y in order to make money with your ideas, knowledge, and experience, especially when you've packaged your wisdom according to the P.R.I.S.M.® system.

You can sell more of your product with less actual "selling" than you ever thought possible.

Here are just a few ideas on how to set up the external money game for your customers so that they feel free to buy from you:

1. Create calls to action

You must also learn how to ask for the behavior you want to elicit – in other words, how to ask for the sale.

It's been my experience that many content providers are reluctant to ask for the sale. As children, most of us were taught two particular behaviors:

Don't talk to strangers

Don't ask for money

The problem is that as entrepreneurs we're in the business of…talking to strangers and asking them for money!

You must master the art of simply asking for the sale. It doesn't have to be complicated, and it certainly doesn't need to be manipulative.

It can be as simple as this: "Can you see how this would be a good fit for you at this particular point in your life? If so, let's go ahead and get started."

This is not a sales book, so I'm not going to teach you how to do "sales pitches." I will tell you this.

When you apply my P.R.I.S.M.™ system to your communications and you represent yourself through video in a powerful way, you'll find "closing techniques" and "psychological sales tactics" are virtually unnecessary. Selling will begin to happen by itself naturally.

2. Ask for the sale more often.

Find different ways to ask for the sale. It doesn't have to be overt or pushy. It could be subtle, such as when I mention that I have one–on–one consulting relationships with clients.

That's actually an invitation for you to engage me in such a relationship if you feel it's appropriate. Or perhaps you may mention that you have workshops that are available for small groups of people. These are "calls to action," albeit very subtle.

3. Over – deliver by giving your best material away for free.

Over – delivering precedes you getting money, because it demonstrates your value before you even ask for a transaction. Often this will result in people asking how they can spend money with you before you even propose the idea yourself.

4. Position for higher value.

One of the things you need to overcome in any business that involves teaching, coaching, consulting, products or books is the temptation to under – price or be the cheapest solution.

It's important that you establish your preeminence in the field and you position yourself for higher value. After all, which car would you rather drive – a Kia or a Mercedes Benz?

Now, is a Mercedes Benz that much more reliable than a Kia, or will they both get you to your destination reliably and safely in the same period of time?

We both know the answer is both cars fulfill their function pretty much the same way. However, the perception is that the Mercedes Benz is of higher value, and that is not by accident. It is a brand position purposefully constructed by the Mercedes Benz company.

5. Communicate for sales

You need to learn to master the art of sales communication – in other words, the artful elegant ways to ask for money. You might start by reading a few good sales books or taking a few good courses on selling. Studying copywriting for sales will not only help you write better video sales scripts, it will assist you with the structure for all types of videos. Sales is the process of influencing your viewer to purchase. Whether you think you are selling or not, every video you create should be influencing your viewer to some specific action.

Go to wisdomography.com/prism – resources for a list of the sales training courses I am currently recommending.

So now you've been through the entire P.R.I.S.M.™ system applied to video. You understand the power of a Purpose – driven business. You know that it's necessary to connect with the purpose of your audience and help them meet their own deep psychological needs. That's what will drive them to watch your videos and purchase your products.

You've learned the danger of the Resistance, and how it can stop you from living your Purpose. You know how things like time, value, technology, complexity and lack of trust can stop people from receiving your message openly.

You've learned the power of Influence to sell without selling, how psychological triggers, anchors, and associations make receiving your communications a must, and can actually make hearing from you a habit or a positive addiction for your audience.

You understand the ultimate value of Systems, so that your business can run in a way that is efficient and affordable as people visit and hear your message through online video.

And finally, you know the methods by which you can turn your message into Money.

So what's next? Before we get to that, I'd like to cover why video – based communications mastery is critical to your success. That's what we'll do in the next chapter.

A QUOTE
WORTH NOTE

MONEY IS THE
ACCELERANT FOR THE
FIRE THAT SPREADS
YOUR MESSAGE.

Debz

VISUAL PROCESSING DOMINATION

Chapter 7

Video: Your Most Effective Communications Tool

Visual processing doesn't just assist in the perception of our world. It dominates the perception of our world.

John Medina

We all want our greatest contributions, our unique wisdom to be consumed, remembered and acted upon. You will not change the world if you don't communicate your message effectively. And the most effective way to communicate with the human brain is visually.

Brain researchers have known for more than 100 years about the pictorial superiority effect: "the more visual the input becomes, the more likely it is to be recognized – and recalled" (check out Brain Rules by John Medina for the scientific scoop). Visual data is processed 60,000 times faster by the brain than text.

Time to Process Data

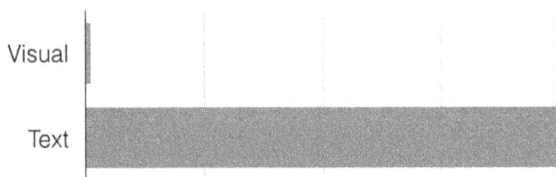

Visual data are processed 60,000 times faster than text

In fact, only ten percent of Information presented orally is remembered 72 hours later. Add a picture and suddenly sixty – five percent is remembered. Because the brain first turns text into pictures, it processes the written word more slowly than pictures. When reading, most of us attempt to visualize what the text is telling us.

% Remembered after 72 Hours

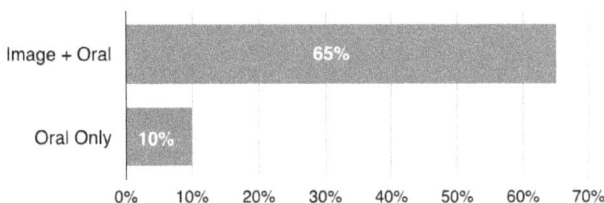

Only ten percent of Information presented orally is
remembered 72 hours later.
While sixty-five percent is remembered if you add a picture.

Color, orientation, size, brightness, and especially motion and emotion are the things that attract our attention. That's where video takes the lead.

The brain also likes multi – sensory experiences and video, created from a great script designed to move your viewers emotionally is one of the best ways to stimulate the visual (sight), auditory (sound) and kinesthetic (touch/feeling) senses. If you're really good, you can stimulate your audience to experience the olfactory (smell) and gustatory (taste) senses as well.

Online Video Value

"We tend to trust humans, not some corporate logo; and video is the best way to do that on a scaled basis."

– Frank Eliason, senior vice president, Citibank.

The effectiveness of video has been the subject of business research ever since the bandwidth of the Internet became large enough for the masses to watch streaming video online.

Take a look at the power of video defined by these statistics. (Statistics sources are in the Appendix.)

What Online Video Means for You

Video results in a 75% increase in understanding & application of information.

80% of all Internet users watch video.

Web visitors who view a product video are 85% more likely to make a purchase

Videos on landing pages increase conversions by 86%

Inserting "video" into an email subject line improves click through rates by 7% to 13%

Embedding a video in the body improves conversion rates more than 20%

Posting videos throughout your website invites 2-3 times more traffic, doubles stick time, increases organic search traffic by more than 150%.

75% decrease in subscriber opt-outs when a video was included in an introductory email

"In the age of infobesity and increasing digital noise, visual storytelling has emerged as a strategy for not only standing out, but also for nurturing and growing vibrant and engaged communities. The ability to craft visuals that inspire emotion and action is helping companies to be noticed and is amplifying their stories through those communities.

Attention is the new commodity. Visual storytelling is the new currency."

– Ekaterina Walter and Jessica Gioglio, authors of
The Power of Visual Storytelling.

Is it by accident that 81% of marketers use video in marketing activities? No, because it's the fastest way for experts and thought leaders to establish their brand and get noticed. What are you waiting for?

Do you feel intimidated? Are you not sure what it takes to create quality, effective video?

Take a deep breath. In the next chapter, we'll go over some of the biggest mistakes that people tend to make when communicating through video.

A QUOTE
WORTH NOTE

Video is the easiest and most efficient method of engaging your audience, gaining trust and building your brand.

Debz

10 BIGGEST MISTAKES TO AVOID

2. DAZED & CONFUSED

1. TURTLE TIME

3. DESIGNED FOR THE BLIND

5. ANNOYING AUDIO

4. LACKLUSTER PERFORMANCE

6. WITNESS PROTECTION LIGHTING

7. DISTRACTING BACKGROUND

9. FLAWED FINISHING

8. NAUSEATING MOVEMENT

10. COUSIN CHARLIE

BONUS UPRIGHT SMARTPHONE

Chapter 8

The 10 Biggest Mistakes to Avoid

A man must be big enough to admit his mistakes, smart enough to profit from them, and strong enough to correct them.

John Maxwell

There are many pitfalls to avoid in this business of yours. Interestingly, I see people making the same mistakes over and over again when it comes to communicating their message powerfully through video.

A mistake made once is an opportunity to learn; the same mistake made again, wasted opportunity.

Here are the 10 biggest mistakes people make when trying to communicate with video:

1. Turtle Time

Video games, the proliferation of the Internet, ADD… whatever the reason, it is now believed that our attention spans have been reduced to less than seconds. We have adapted to wanting our content in small doses. Statistics show that most online video viewership drops off after 60 seconds. Your favorite TV shows typically break for commercials after five to seven minutes of content.

If you want your message consumed, especially by those who have encountered your message for the first time, keep your video durations to three minutes or less. Practice getting a great tip across in 60 seconds or less.

Your audience's time is very valuable to them. They are trading their time for value from you and your message. Don't abuse their trust.

Once your audience gets to know, like and trust you, they will stay engaged for longer content videos up to ten minutes. The longer your video is, the more time you need to spend in editing to keep your audience engaged. Keep it tight and eliminate opportunities for boredom.

Unless you are creating videos for the 70+ crowd, slow and steady content does not win the video consumption race. Create content for rabbits, not turtles.

2. Dazed and Confused

Many people try to cover too much ground in a single video which may be one reason why so many videos are too long. Keep focused on the one thing you want your audience to take away from your video. Clarity is power.

Confusion will only lead to inaction, and action is the reason you are creating the video in the first place: to buy, to subscribe, to share, to learn more on your website, etc.)

Break long videos into a series of single – focused chunks to make them more consumable. Give your videos a structure and try to be consistent when possible. Balance creating certainty and variety. Let your audience know what to expect from you, and then add in a few unexpected surprises.

Use the P.R.I.S.M.™ framework to clarify your core message. Connect emotionally, not just with facts and data. Use storytelling to back up your core message to make it more memorable. And remember your Call to Action. Don't leave them confused about what to do next.

3. Designed for the Blind

Here's a question for you to think about: if your core message can be understood just as well by listening to your video's audio track, why are you creating a video? Plopping yourself in front of the camera and just talking away is nothing more than a podcast with a moving photo. In video, the mantra is always: "Show, don't tell."

The medium of video is incredibly powerful. Think beyond the "talking head" style video and add some other visuals: photos, graphics, live props, or visually descriptive video to enhance and reinforce your message. Consider a mini – documentary style with a story arc that captivates the attention of your audience.

4. Lackluster Performance

The sweat is trickling down your face. Your hands are fidgeting. You have no energy. You are constantly shifting your weight and swaying back and forth. Even though you really know your subject, every other word comes out as "uh" or "you know."

Yes, I understand that you are not trained to be on camera (at least not yet), but a distracting performance on camera detracts from your message no matter how brilliant it is. So it's time to practice – with the camera on! You have to get comfortable and be able to relax on camera. Smile. The audience on the other side of your camera lens really wants to know and like you.

No, you don't have to be perfect (we covered that in Chapter 3). But you do need to project confidence, trustworthiness and expertise.

Here's an exercise to help you build up your confidence right before filming begins. Stand with your feet shoulder width apart, with your weight evenly distributed, with your hands on your hips, your head held high, and your shoulders back. Breathe deep and slow with a smile on your face. At the same time, think of an experience in your past when you felt really confident. Do this for five to ten minutes before you go on camera. Believe it or not, this physicality actually changes your body chemistry. To learn more about how this happens, watch Amy Cuddy's TED talk, *Your Body Language Shapes Who You Are.*

5. Annoying Audio

Any professional videographer or filmmaker will tell you that the most important technical aspect of video is *audio*. People will still watch a poorly lit video or even a blank screen if the audio is clear and the content is interesting or entertaining. However, few people will watch even a well lit, well composed video for more than a few seconds if the audio is too distorted, too staticky, too quiet, or too full of background noise.

If you are just starting out to create videos, your first investment should be a good external microphone. Never rely on the built – in mics found on smartphones, webcams, consumer/prosumer video cameras or HDLSR cameras. The closer the mic is to the sound source (that means your mouth), the better the audio quality will be.

A lavalier microphone (often called a "lav") is a good choice. Check out our online resources guide for the most up – to – date information on lav mics and how to use them correctly at http://wisdomography.com/prism–resources.

Also, be sure to listen to your environment for distracting sounds: air conditioning fans, refrigerator hums, traffic noise, excessive echo, animals, kids, etc. The best way to hear them is through over the ear headphones attached to your camera or audio recording device.

Choose a location that reduces these distractions as much as possible. Your viewers will thank you with better attention to your message.

6. Witness Protection Lighting

The human brain is attracted to faces. That includes yours if you are doing a live video. Be sure to have enough light on your face so the viewers can see the sparkle in your eyes – that's where the human connection is made.

The light on you should be brighter than the light on your background. Avoid light that is directly overhead – it will create dark shadows under your eyes. Avoid light shining up from below you – that's like holding a flashlight under your chin to tell a scary story. Avoid shooting your video in front of a window during the day, unless you want that witness protection program silhouette look.

If you are relying on sunlight from a window, position the window to your side at a 45 – 60 degree angle. A sheer curtain on the window will help to diffuse the light creating a larger light source with a softer more flattering light on your face.

7. Distracting Background

Congratulations! You just spent three hours shooting the most incredible videos of your life. Everything was just right – your core message, your energy, your confidence, your delivery, the audio, the lighting. You couldn't be more proud. You play back the video for your best friend so you can gloat, and then you see it. There in your background just behind your head is last night's empty tequila bottle, bags of junk food and dirty socks draped over the sofa.

Unless you are spoofing a Saturday Night Live skit, this may not be the image you wanted to project to your viewers. It's easy enough to move all of those items out of the way now, but the last three hours of your life were just wasted. Make it a habit to check the environment before you start recording. Really look through the camera lens or viewfinder and check all the sides and corners for those unwanted surprises.

Even if you don't have embarrassing items in your background, it's still good to declutter and remove any distractions from your background. Everything in your video frame should have a purpose. Everything in your frame should support or enhance your message and your brand. If not, remove it.

8. Nauseating Camera Movement

Handheld video? Please kids, don't try this at home.

Handheld cameras have their place in video production… in the hands of experienced professionals. It takes the right support systems and a lot of practice to shoot handheld without creating distraction or worse, nausea.

Please, get a tripod – even an inexpensive one. Enough said. Your viewers will thank you.

9. Flawed Finishing

An effective video is not finished until it is edited. You or your assistant should be able to handle the simple edits for your quickie 60 second tip videos – just add in your branding and call to action graphics. Create a template in your video editing software to ensure consistency and quality.

When you begin producing more involved videos, outsource the editing. Sure you may be able to learn how to do it yourself, but is that the best use of your valuable time? An experienced editor can make you look better and make your video more effective in less time than you ever could.

But wait… there's more. You are not finished with your video until it is available for others to see. Create a checklist for distribution. Make sure you have appropriate titles, keywords, tags, descriptions, and transcripts. This is another area that is good to outsource.

10. Cousin with a Camera

So you're ready to move beyond the smartphone/webcam quickie tip video and really create a quality intro or about video that you can use for years to come. Your first thought is "I'll save some money and get my Cousin Charlie to help me."

Let me ask you a question. What is your time worth? True, Cousin Charlie is free, but he is also the poster boy for "you get what you pay for." Whether you work with Cousin Charlie or hire experienced professionals, you are still putting in your time to create the video – and in some cases a lot more of your time with Cousin Charlie. If Cousin Charlie isn't a video professional or at least willing to get training, you may end up with a video that downgrades your brand, devalues your message and has completely wasted your valuable time.

When you are ready to step up the value of your message and brand, invest in quality production with professionals. It will save you more time, money and stress in the long run.

11. BONUS Mistake: The Upright Smartphone

You are habituated to holding your smartphone like a phone... vertically. Then you decide to shoot a quick video on your phone in the spur of the moment. You find the camera app, making sure you hit the record button and what do you do? Yep, you're holding it vertically again while capturing video.

Have you noticed that you always watch a movie with your phone turned horizontally? That's because video is a wide format, not a tall format. Maybe this is just a pet peeve of mine, but seriously, does anyone want to watch a tiny video with large black bars on both sides? That's how a video captured vertically will play back online.

Nothing screams amateur more than a vertical video. So next time you grab your smartphone to shoot a video, remember to hold it horizontally. I (and your viewing public) will thank you!

Okay, now that you know what to avoid, what do you actually do? What are the next steps? That's what Chapter 9 is all about...what to do now.

A QUOTE
WORTH NOTE

A MISTAKE MADE ONCE
IS AN OPPORTUNITY TO
LEARN; THE SAME
MISTAKE MADE AGAIN
WASTED OPPORTUNITY.

Debz

WHAT NOW?
IT'S TIME TO SHARE
YOUR WISDOM!

Chapter 9

What to Do Now:
The 30 – Day Challenge

The secret of concentration is the secret of self – discovery.
You reach inside yourself to discover your personal
resources, and what it takes to match them to the challenge.

Arnold Palmer

We've been through a lot together. We've covered the basic steps of the P.R.I.S.M.™ system. We've understood the Wisdomography Value Pyramid of content creation, and I've walked you through how to develop your videos in such a way that they are more powerful, more persuasive, more influential, and will produce more profits for you.

Here's what I know from experience. It's quite possible for me to have communicated all this information to you, and for you to have read it, understood it, and nodded sagely as you did so.

It's possible that you took lots of notes, that you did lots of underlining, actually answered the questions I posed, and that you've made a promise to yourself that this time you're going to move forward. It's also possible that you may find it difficult to proceed from here.

For one reason or another (life happens), you may not actually see any change as a result of having read this book. This is not the book's fault, and up until now it's not been your fault either. But now that you know the barriers that stand in the way of your powerful communication and visual impact of your message, what will you do? Now it's your responsibility to do things differently than you've done them in the past.

I'd like to issue a 30 – day challenge for you. My challenge is simply this: Put the P.R.I.S.M.™ system into action. Structure your video – based communications around the P.R.I.S.M.™ acronym.

Make sure that your videos...

are structured with	**P**urpose,
overcome	**R**esistance,
are designed to	**I**nfluence
are	**S**ystematic
and set up to produce	**M**oney

Use the psychological principles that you've learned to communicate your message in a way that helps your prospects and customers overcome those barriers as well.

Go back through the book and make notes about how you're going to practically apply the steps to your own business and your own communications. After you've done that, map out a plan over the next 30 days. Make sure that every day you're taking one simple action to move forward in the process of more powerful communication for you and your business.

It might also be a good idea to get direct help or coaching from someone. Often you cannot see your own "bad form" when you're in the process of learning something new.

This is why great golf players like Tiger Woods hire coaches,. Great musicians, great ballet performer, great artists and great business people do the same thing. This is why I recommend that you employ a coach or consultant or video professional as well, to help you accelerate your progress in your field.

It's true, I might be perceived as being somewhat self – serving in this message because I offer direct coaching for a limited number of clients in the art of impactful video communication.

I also do small – group workshops, which are more affordable and help you craft your own video messaging in a way that follows the P.R.I.S.M™ system to the T. But whether you get help from me or from someone else, get some external coaching to help you see the mistakes you're making and the areas where you need improvement.

Whatever you do, make this commitment to use the techniques and principles you've learned in this book to move forward and make progress over the next 30 days.

Make the commitment to use the P.R.I.S.M.™ system to display the rainbow of light and illumination that you bring to the world, to bring more vibrant color to the rest of us, to show us the value that you create, that you were designed to deliver, and that you're fulfilling as your destiny. I don't expect anything less from you.

~ Debz

A QUOTE
WORTH NOTE

NOW THAT YOU KNOW
THE BARRIERS THAT
STAND IN THE WAY
OF POWERFULLY
COMMUNICATING YOUR
WISDOM, IT'S YOUR
RESPONSIBILITY TO DO
THINGS DIFFERENTLY
THAN YOU'VE DONE
THEM IN THE PAST.

Debz

Appendix A

Resources and Recommendations

An investment in knowledge pays the best interest.

Benjamin Franklin

Visit http://wisdomography.com/prism – resources for the most up – to – date information and websites on the topics covered in this book.

Below I have provided a list that you may find useful in furthering your understanding of each topic.

Purpose

Tony Robbins' TED Talk: *Why We Do What We Do*

The Purpose Economy by Aaron Hurst

Resistance

The War of Art by Steven Pressfield

The Power of Habit by Charles Duhigg

Influence

Influence: Science and Practice by Robert Cialdini

Made to Stick by Chip Heath and Dan Heath

Contagious by Jonah Berger

Systems

Switch by Chip Heath and Dan Heath

Work the System by Sam Carpenter

Pomodoro Technique by Francesco Cirillo

Who by Jeffery Smart – getting A players on your team

Money

The Ultimate Blueprint for an Insanely Successful Business by Keith Cunningham

The $100 Startup by Chris Guillebeau

Visual Communications Mastery

The Power of Visual Storytelling by Ekaterina Walter and Jessica Gioglio

Lead with a Story by Paul Smith

The Presentation Secrets of Steve Jobs by Carmine Gallo

The Art of Explanation by Lee Lefever

And of course…

> http://wisdomography.com/prism-resources for guides
> to content creation, scripting, performance and technical
> aspects of Video Communications Mastery

Online Video Statistics Sources:

Hubspot.com, MarketingTechBlog.com,
eMarketer.com, WebDamSolutions.com,
Salesforce.com, InternetRetailer.com, ReelSEO.com,
ContentMarketingInstitute.com, VisibleMeasures.com,
Forbes.com, VideoBrewery.com, Quicksprout.com,
MOS.com, MarketingShrepa.com, SwitchVideo.com,
Forrester.com, Experian.com, Invodo.com

Get Free Info – Graphics

Download these free, printable charts that help you become a better Visual Communicator at my website: wisdomography.com/prism-resources

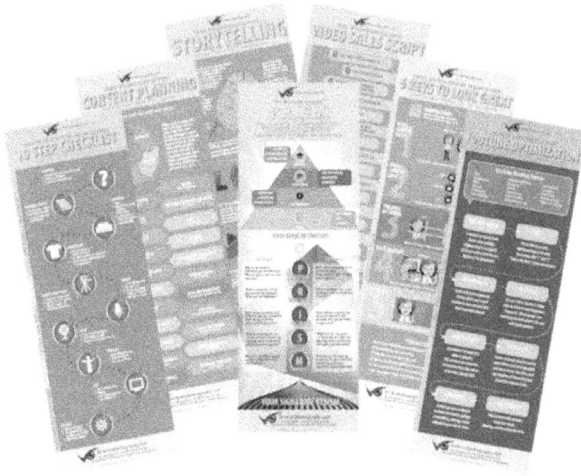

- **Create Influential On – Camera Video: 10 – Step Checklist**

- Content Planning: When You Don't Know What To Shoot

- **Storytelling: Maximum Persuasion in Minimum Time**

- Video Sales Script: 21 Steps To a Killer Sales Video

- **5 Keys To Looking Great On Camera**

- The *Wisdomography P.R.I.S.M® System* On One Page

Get FREE Exposure By

Partnering With Google

Download this Guide <u>NOW</u> at
<u>Wisdomography.com/extend</u>

YOU Can Present On–Camera Like A Seasoned Pro

Download This eBook NOW at
Wisdomography.com/power

www.ingramcontent.com/pod-product-compliance
Lightning Source LLC
Chambersburg PA
CBHW032005190326
41520CB00007B/366